D1162201

A Heart Full of Happiness

of

CELEBRATING THE JOY OF CONTENTMENT

Alda Ellis

Harvest House Publishers
Eugene, Oregon

A Heart Full of Happiness
Copyright © 2000 by Alda Ellis
Published by Harvest House Publishers
Eugene, OR 97402

Library of Congress Cataloging-in-Publication Data
Ellis, Alda, 1952-
    A heart full of happiness / Alda Ellis.
        p. cm.
    ISBN 0-7369-0334-8
        1. Happiness. I. Title.

    BJ1481 .E55 2000
    248.4—dc21

                                            00-025341

Artwork which appears in this book is from
the personal collection of Alda Ellis.

Design and production by Left Coast Design, Portland, Oregon

Scripture quotations are from the Holy Bible, New
International Version ®. Copyright © 1973, 1978,
1984 by the International Bible Society. Used by
permission of Zondervan Publishing House.

Dedication

To my supportive
husband and to our
two sons, Samuel and
Mason, who have
filled my heart
with happiness

Contents

Heart of Joy

Whoever is happy will make others happy too.
ANNE FRANK

I was out antiquing with a friend one day when we stopped at an estate sale to observe a display of cherished objects. Cheerful kitchen glasses, well-worn mixing bowls, a varied selection of cookie cutters, and hand-crocheted hot pads sat artfully arranged on a table. I knew instantly that whomever these things had belonged to had fulfilled her days by lovingly caring for family and friends. Another grouping of items displayed on a dresser included a pair of white gloves, a strand of pearls, and a silver monogrammed hand mirror. Several birthday, Mother's Day, and all-occasion correspondence cards were bundled together, tied up cheerfully with a pink satin ribbon. As I admired these treasures, I felt as if my friend and I were peering through a window into someone's life.

A young lady straightening and tidying up the area with a feather duster greeted us. She explained that her grandmother had passed away and that she and her mother were now selling her possessions to someone who might find pleasure in them, too.

As I admired a lovely brooch, the granddaughter told us the story of how her grandmother had purchased the brooch as a souvenir from her trip to St. Louis—her first-ever journey by automobile. Although the granddaughter and her mother adored these heirlooms, their tiny rented apartment simply did not have enough room to hold everything. Now here, in a modest ten-foot space, the portrait of a beautiful life was revealed. Seeing those treasures and imagining that grand lady's life so long ago set my mind to dreaming.

I just love to ramble through estate sales, tag sales, and antique shops, especially those located in out-of-the-way places. The glimpses I receive of hard times in years past make me so thankful for all of the niceties and conveniences we are blessed with today. My observations garnered from my antique sojourns always persist in my mind and cause me to ponder deeper things. For instance, I've learned that making a living is not necessarily the same thing as making a life. I've also discovered that the essence of a happy and contented life is hard to define—and even harder to grasp. I think that there are certain things we must do to create a heart full of happiness.

Back when I was a college student, I fretted over just what *things* would guarantee that my life be a happy one. At the time, I thought that certainly my new car would assure me of happiness, but it eventually grew old. Maybe the answer was a new outfit. But it soon went out of style. Yet somehow volunteering in the dental health van that

traveled to underprivileged schools made me very happy and content.

It took me years to realize that if I searched to find the "something" that was the secret to my own happiness, it was quite elusive. But if I concentrated on what I could do to help others, I quickly found joy for myself. The secret to contentment was all in my attitude. I could either tally up all the things I did not have, or I could count all the blessings I possessed—gifts that money cannot buy such as good health, a strong faith, and a loving family. My treasures were perhaps only wishes for most people, even for great kings. And what a wonderfully firm foundation I have to build my life upon.

Something to love, something to do, something to enjoy, and something to hope for. These treasures are as timeless now as they ever were. My something to love is certainly my family. My something to do is nurturing and caring for family, friends, and home and running my business. My something to hope for is my faith that sees me through good times and bad. These are the secrets to happiness that are most treasured in my soul.

My crown is in my heart, not on my head,
Not decked with diamonds, and Indian stones,
Nor to be seen: my crown is called Content;
A crown it is that seldom Kings enjoy.
WILLIAM SHAKESPEARE

CHAPTER ONE

The Happiness of Family and Friends

*Friendship is a word the very sight
of which in print makes the heart warm.*

AUGUSTINE BIRRELL

Camping is an activity that I have never been particularly good at, but as the mother of two boys, I've learned to enjoy it. Every October, we go on a family camping trip with a truckload of gear and our canoe mounted atop our Suburban. We head into the mountains about four hours away from home. Breathing in the clean mountain air and soaking in the stunning colors of autumn leaves against the bright blue sky is something I dearly look forward to all year long. We have set up camp in the same familiar spot, way back in the woods, for several years now, but we make new discoveries upon each return. Hiking, fishing, and canoeing fill our weekend, and I love awakening to the aroma of my husband's pancakes on the cookstove.

I awoke this morning with devout thanksgiving for my friends.
RALPH WALDO EMERSON

One year, while hiking down a dirt road on a rugged limestone bluff, we happened upon an old family cemetery shaded by a canopy of cedars. Some of the tombstones were tilted with age, the heavy marble shaded with lichen. The dates on some monuments were faded and difficult to read, but most dated back to the late 1800s and early 1900s. One had a little lamb figurine carved out of the top of the stone, and below it were the birth and death dates of a young child. As we read the inscriptions on the stones, we knew that these had been beloved husbands and wives, mothers and fathers.

Wherever I go, I carry paper and pencil with me, so I copied down an inscription I found carved on one of the crumbling monuments:

*Spring will come again
to the valley,
Flowers will come again
in the spring,
And the Shepherd will
return for His sheep.*

Back at our campsite, we huddled around a campfire and gazed at the stars as the day drew to a close. The crackle of the flames rewarded our senses as the smoke curled upward. Hands locked behind our heads, we leaned back in our chairs to gaze at the countless stars brightening the clear

The Treasures of a Lifetime

I like to keep my best-loved treasures in my studio, where I can gaze at them, reflect, remember, and dream. As you look at my list of cherished objects, think of the things in your own life that you hold dear. Place them somewhere where you, too, can gaze at them with a joyful heart.

- a plaster-of-Paris mold of my son's hand
- a recipe for spice apple cake, written in my grandmother's handwriting
- a baby quilt, hand-stitched by my great-grandmother
- my mother's green teapot that she made tea in every day
- my wedding ring
- our family Bible, with births, deaths, and marriages dutifully recorded

night sky. The still quiet of the evening was every so often broken by laughter and reflection. It was hard to leave the warm glow of the fire and turn toward the tent, but the chipped blue enamel coffeepot had grown empty and the night had gotten cold.

A good deed is never lost; he who sows courtesy reaps friendship, and he who plants kindness gathers love.
ST. BASIL

It is perhaps in the quiet of the mountains that I best realize what a gift each and every day is, blessed as I am with family, home, work, and faith. For I know in my heart that just as the sun rises, it also sets, and the Shepherd will return for His sheep.

A few years ago, four friends and I traveled to London in search of antiques. We had cleared our busy schedules in order to enjoy time together amid the alleys of antique silver and one-of-a-kind discoveries. In search of shopkeepers' treasures, the real rewards we brought home were renewed friendships and fond memories of our time together.

Our flight arrived at Heathrow airport very early on a cold Sunday morning in February. The train at Victoria Station carried us to our hotel, where we checked into our charming, authentically English rooms. Settling in didn't take long. Just a quick splash of water to refresh our faces and a moment spent hanging up a few garments, and we were ready to begin exploring.

Although it took quite a bit of effort to plan the trip and fit it into all of our schedules, we decided that we did not wish to have a formal itinerary for our time in England. We would take each day as an adventure all its own. We did, however, have a few points of interest we all wanted to visit. On our collective "must-see" list was the magnificent St. Paul Cathedral in the heart of the city. As we arrived on a Sunday, we decided to visit it first.

Ways to Say, "You're Special!"

- When sending a greeting card to a friend or loved one, surprise them with sprinkles of confetti or glitter in the envelope.
- Start your own tradition of including the entire family in birthday and holiday decorating and baking.
- Place a note that says, "I love you" in your child's lunch box.
- Surprise a friend with a blooming African violet for her desk.
- Leave your husband an "I love you" note in his sock drawer.
- Travel in your car with the radio off. Children will open up in the silence, and it is easier for them to listen to you.
- Plant a tree on a child's birthday and watch it grow together.
- Leave a borrowed car with a full tank of gas.
- Plant zinnias in your garden. You'll always be able to give someone flowers.
- Go on a picnic, even if it is just peanut butter and jelly sandwiches at the park.
- Pack a bag of brownies for a friend or family member going on a trip.
- Make sure everyone in the car is wearing seat belts.
- Hold hands and watch the sun set with someone special.
- Frame a picture of you and your friend together and send it to her.
- Put up a front porch swing, a rope swing, a tree swing, or a tire swing.
- Send your neighbor homemade soup for no reason at all.
- Start a tradition of a family dinner together on Sunday evenings.

All five of us piled into a London taxi, and the driver let us out in front of the cathedral on a corner aflutter with pigeons. St. Paul's stood before us, a monument in the sky, its steeple pointing to the gray clouds above. Pulling up our collars to protect ourselves from the wind, we observed for a moment the people going in the massive doors. And then up the three hundred and ninety-seven gray steps we climbed. Upon reaching the foyer, we were met by an usher who showed us where we could sit in on the service. We walked up the long aisle single file to join the congregation of faithful parishioners. The organ played as the boys' choir sang behind the altar rail. Taking off our coats, we nestled into our pew and turned to the correct page in the hymnal to join in the singing.

> *You built no great cathedrals*
> *That centuries applaud,*
> *But with a grace exquisite*
> *Your life cathedraled God.*
> THOMAS FESSENDEN

After the service, we had the pleasure of touring the grand cathedral. A knowledgeable volunteer shared with us the history of the Great Fire of London in 1666 and how, afterward, the talented architect Sir Christopher Wren began the process of designing

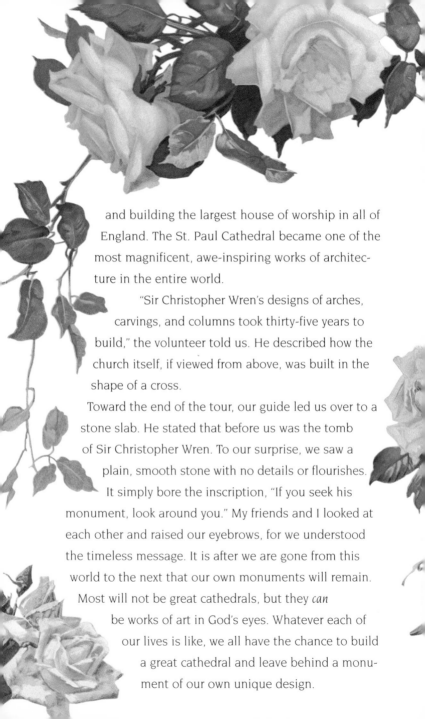

and building the largest house of worship in all of England. The St. Paul Cathedral became one of the most magnificent, awe-inspiring works of architecture in the entire world.

"Sir Christopher Wren's designs of arches, carvings, and columns took thirty-five years to build," the volunteer told us. He described how the church itself, if viewed from above, was built in the shape of a cross.

Toward the end of the tour, our guide led us over to a stone slab. He stated that before us was the tomb of Sir Christopher Wren. To our surprise, we saw a plain, smooth stone with no details or flourishes. It simply bore the inscription, "If you seek his monument, look around you." My friends and I looked at each other and raised our eyebrows, for we understood the timeless message. It is after we are gone from this world to the next that our own monuments will remain. Most will not be great cathedrals, but they *can* be works of art in God's eyes. Whatever each of our lives is like, we all have the chance to build a great cathedral and leave behind a monument of our own unique design.

"Take your needle, my child, and work at your pattern; it will come out a rose by and by." Life is like that; one stitch at a time taken patiently, and the pattern will come out all right like embroidery.

OLIVER WENDELL HOLMES

I hope that my cathedral is the legacy I leave this world through my two sons. I will never forget the words of my dear friend Sharon, who noticed how frazzled I was one day. She put her arm around me and asked what was wrong. I told her that I simply needed more hours in my day. Sharon is blessed with the gift of listening, and so I poured out my heart to her. I shared how trying to fit my volunteer work, my sons' music lessons, ball games, and school play practices, and my own job responsibilities into my schedule was causing such a strain on my family and on myself. I explained that because I was so blessed, I felt I needed to give something back to my community. Sharon gently reminded me that for everything there is a season and asked, "What is top priority in your life?" My answer was easy. "It is being a wife and a mother."

Sharon's wise words rang clear. The best thing I could "give back" to my community was the gift of two fine young men. That very day, I went home and wrote letters of resignation to the boards of organizations I volunteered for. I felt such peace after I wrote those letters, like a ton of bricks had been lifted off my back. My focus had returned to my family.

I'm glad I made that decision, for all too soon, my sons will be off to college. It is my prayer that I have forged a relationship of love and trust with them, and that they have forged such a relationship with our Heavenly Father. My responsibility was to plant seeds of goodness and strength in their souls and to nurture them. The lessons I have taught them will someday greatly influence their life decisions. The day will come when I will have an empty house and a desperate need to fill my days. Then I will again become active in the causes that I so believe in. Just as Sharon reminded me, for everything there is a season.

> *Two are better than one, because they have a good return for their work; if one falls down, his friend can help him up.*
> THE BOOK OF ECCLESIASTES

I like the idea of marking seasons and milestones with traditions. One of the traditions that my mother left me with is that of really *celebrating* family birthdays. When my sister and I were little, we were blessed and showered with gifts, despite a very frugal family budget. These gifts were not necessarily ones that money could buy. More importantly, they were gifts of a day made special just for us. Our birthday celebrations usually included a new home-made dress. It was generally something we needed anyway, but it made the school day ever so special. And all day long we looked forward to the evening birthday meal—a family dinner made elegant with candles and our Sunday dishes. Birthday napkins at each place setting added a festive touch. A few balloons from the dime store danced in the doorway, and birthday cards from friends lined up on the kitchen windowsill.

Mother was a wonderful cook, and she showcased her talents on our birthday cakes. When I was little, I always longed for one of those fancy bakery cakes with white icing and red roses. Now I long for one of Mother's fresh apple cakes frosted with caramel icing. I have fond memories of sitting on the kitchen stool, patiently watching her frost the cake. Somehow she always ended up with a little too much icing, so she left it in the mixing bowl and handed it to me along with a wooden spoon and a smile.

My sister and I have tried to carry on the tradition of making birthdays special, even though we are both working mothers. It is the little ways of saying, "I love you" that make a birthday celebration—or any celebration—for a child, husband, or friend, full of love. That is the most wonderful thing about traditions. They make you feel loved and part of a family, part of a group of friends, and part of something very special. Sharing ourselves and our talents with family and friends is a legacy of love and happiness that we can leave to the world.

CHAPTER TWO

The Happiness of Home

To build a house is one thing, but to make it a home is quite another.

LOUIS L'AMOUR

Years ago, my husband and I were on our way out of town when we saw something that made us slow our car and stop in disbelief. An historical home that we had passed by often during our growing-up days, a home that had once been a regal landmark but had since fallen into disrepair, had a "For Sale" sign on the front lawn. Looking past the broken windows and creaky porch boards, we decided to take a peek inside. Upon entering, we stepped over the fallen window screens and broken glass lying scattered on the living room floor. The light fixtures had been stripped and a musty smell lingered.

"What in the world were we thinking?" I thought to myself. But that question was answered upon entering the dining room. The setting sun cast a rosy glow on a mural on the wall, a beautiful, hand-painted scene portraying a hillside stream spanned by an enchanting wooden bridge. A winding road led toward a charming little house in the distance. The technique that the unknown artist had used in his painting was an optical illusion, for no matter where I stood in the room, the perspective changed. I was always looking straight down the path going home.

Flowers always make people better, happier; and more helpful; they are sunshine, food and medicine to the soul.
LUTHER BURBANK

My husband and I realized our dream and bought that house. After restoring it to its former self, complete with nooks and crannies, balcony, stairwells, and porch, it has become our own personal haven. It has taken years to get the house looking how it looks now, and it will probably never be considered "finished," for I like my home to have a lived-in, cozy look. I never want it to resemble an austere hotel lobby.

My home is filled with hand-me-down furniture from generations past, a collection of cookbooks, hurricane lamps, and antique dishes. My favorite furnishings are my kitchen chairs, which once belonged to my grandmother. I have such wonderful memories of sitting on them at her

Welcome Home the Senses

When you set out to
create a welcoming home,
be certain to consider
all of the senses—
smell, sight, touch,
taste, and sound.

Smell — Smell is the strongest
of our senses. Scent sends
certain signals to the right side of the brain, the
place where memory, creativity, and emotions reside.
When the fragrance is pleasurable, we associate it with
a sense of well-being. Use candles, fresh flowers, and
potpourri to create a spirit of welcome.

Sight — Strive to keep a tidy home with minimal clutter.
Organization in itself is serene and relaxing. Display cherished
objects rich in meaning, and create little corners of coziness in all of
the rooms.

Touch — "It feels so good to be home." This is what you want people
to think when they walk through the door. Create this welcome-home
feeling by lighting little lamps and omitting strong overhead lighting.
Soft pillows and blankets provide a soothing touch.

Taste — A glass of iced tea or a cup of hot tea, depending on the
season, give joy and delight. For me, a tiny piece of chocolate is always
the perfect teatime companion.

Sound — Sounds can set the mood. I set my stereo to classical music so
I can turn it on the minute I walk through the door. The music allows my
mind to focus and breaks a discomforting quiet. Even though my teenage
son does not choose to play classical music in his own room, he heartily
accepts it as the calming music of home.

table. Upon inheriting the chairs, I had them refinished and needlepointed the seats. My sons now also have grown up with these family treasures, and I hope they someday have fond memories of eating breakfast in them before heading off to school.

A house is made of wood and stone but only love can make a home.
AUTHOR UNKNOWN

We are in the process of creating our own memories, too. When the weather begins to turn chilly, we spend Sunday evenings all bundled up and gathered in a cozy spot in the garden behind the house. A merry fire dances in the terra cotta chimney, where we roast marshmallows as we drink hot chocolate. Warming our hands on the toasty mugs, we share our accomplishments for the week past and our hopes for the one that lies ahead. I think it is the simple act of pulling our family together after all of the going and doing that I value most about this time. After all, the little things in life have the most influence on the bigger things.

For our homes to be places that make our hearts happy when we return from the outside world, they must be places that give us a feeling of inner calmness.

As a wife, mother, and business owner, I know that my home needs to be a stable place where I can organize the details of day-to-day living.

I have created little corners of intimacy for my husband, my children, and my guests to help encourage this feeling of serenity. My favorite corner of intimacy is the bath. A hot bath is my way of closing out everything and finding tranquility. My husband has a favorite plump chair with an afghan draped over the arm and a selection of magazines in a basket nearby. He likes to curl up, read, and nap here. My sons have a table all their own with a basket of markers, drawing paper, and a checkerboard on it. It's not necessarily a place to do homework, but rather a place to imagine, create, and enjoy. My oldest son has his

Recipe for a Happy Kitchen

- ❧ Eliminate counter clutter.
- ❧ Search antique shops for vintage kitchen utensils.
- ❧ Fruit is a quick and healthy snack to keep on hand.
- ❧ Create character by showcasing a collection of family dishes.
- ❧ A chandelier adds formality to an eat-in kitchen.
- ❧ Focus on meaningful and practical—not purely decorative—accessories.
- ❧ Bake an extra dozen cookies to take to a neighbor or shut-in.
- ❧ Dine by candlelight to make family dinners special.
- ❧ Give away unused appliances to make someone else's life easier and your kitchen more spacious.
- ❧ Make time to enjoy meals together. Dine together as a family at least once a week. Put down the newspaper and turn off the television. Share daily happenings and concerns with each other.
- ❧ Create a family tradition of togetherness by saying grace before meals.

own hobby area downstairs where he can run his model trains and let his imagination soar. For friends, I simply try to keep a candle burning in my foyer so that there is a gentle welcome in the air when they arrive. And although I am not the wonderful cook my mother was, I always have a cup of tea ready to greet an unexpected guest. I especially love the raspberry- and peach-flavored teas that turn tea with a friend into an extra-special occasion.

I like to nurture my family by adding little luxuries to our home, like the touch of fresh flowers. They give such charm to a side table filled with cherished keepsakes, such as a pair of baby shoes and a baby cup from days gone by. Flowers on the kitchen table, to accompany even an ordinary evening meal, impart a spirit of graciousness. Fragrant blossoms add indulgence to my bathroom as they gracefully sit on the vanity. And to my studio workspace, flowers lend inspiration.

Sometimes we need to pull out a touch of ingenuity when making our homes places of happiness and welcome. Our first home, for instance, had no official foyer or entryway. The front door opened right into the living room. To create a welcoming spirit, I placed an Oriental rug

> *Our house...had a heart and a soul...it was of us, and we were in its confidence and lived in its grace and in the peace of its benedictions.*
>
> MARK TWAIN

runner upon the hardwood flooring. I also set my girl-hood cedar chest near the front door and hung a large mirror over it. On top of the cedar chest I displayed framed family pictures, a small fern in a terra cotta pot, and a bowl for holding keys and mail. During a party the bowl held floating candles. I added a standing coat rack and created my one-of-a-kind foyer.

Most of us have one room of our home that everyone—family and visitors —sees often. Formal living room, great room, den, or parlor—whatever you wish to call it, this is where the spirit of our home most affects the friends who enter. This gathering place also serves as a

haven to our fami-
lies. It is usually the
best-dressed room in a
house, and a cheerful
gathering place
filled with favorite
books and music,
family treasures,
and comfortable furnish-
ings brings contentment
home to all.

My family's living
room is one we really *live*
in. We have a music corner in
the room with music stand,
chair, and violin, case opened
and ready to play. A plump sofa
provides a cozy spot for reading the
paper and napping on Sunday after-
noons. Across from the sofa, I have
arranged a group of chairs in a cozy cluster,
ready for pleasurable conversation by the fireplace. I display some of my favorite collectibles in
this room, and change them around with the seasons,
keeping the atmosphere fresh and lively.

I think that the way in which we display our collections
adds interest and personality to a room. One of my places
of honor for favorite items is the mantel above the fireplace.
Residing among these treasures are a special teacup

given to me by a dear friend, a mantel clock that belonged to my mother, and a black porcelain doorknob from the log cabin my father was born in. I like things that have meaning, things that are not simply some object to fill a space. Things with meaning make my home *mine*.

Perhaps a family's best memories are made in the kitchen. A warm, welcoming place for family and friends to gather and eat is the heart of a home. A glass of ice-cold lemonade in the summer and a cup of fresh apple cider in the fall offer simple hospitality. I like having an informal kitchen that meets my family's needs and encourages friendly interaction. After all, it's easy for me to sweep traces of mud from boys' boots off of my checkerboard floor. A little extra housework in exchange

A Word of Grace
Thank you for the world so sweet,
Thank you for the food we eat,
Thank you for the birds that sing,
Thank you, God, for everything.
And help me to do good on my spelling test.
Amen.

SAMUEL'S BLESSING, AGE 10

for treasured moments with my children is certainly more than a fair tradeoff.

I have learned that one sure way to make a home a happy one is to give thanks for the blessings that reside within its walls. Somehow even a fast food burger, fries,

and milkshake seem like more of a complete meal if we stop and take a moment to say grace. Before we eat, we take turns as family members and guests—if they are comfortable doing so—in saying a prayer of thanksgiving. This is the moment of my day that brings me the most peace and contentment, as I give thanks for the blessings of home and family that I hold most dear.

Although I adore spending time with family and friends, sometimes I need a moment alone to refresh myself. Over time, our bathroom has evolved into a bliss-ful place with room-like furnishings and appointments. When my husband and I remodeled it, we softened the look of the cold porcelain fixtures by adding a mahogany sideboard fitted with a marble top and sink. For a back-board, we used a wonderful old mirror that added sparkle to the surroundings.

> *Happiness is a thing to be practiced, like the violin...*
> SIR JOHN LUBBOCK

Recently, my husband surprised me with long-stemmed red roses for our wedding anniversary. I placed them in a sparkling cut-crystal vase and set them in front of the bathroom mirror. I so enjoyed those roses as I began my day and again as I readied for bed at night. Their fragrance was intensified by the steam of the room. They provided such a lovely splash of color, and when the petals started to fade, they began to fall on the countertop. To enjoy them even further, I sprinkled rose petals in my bath water for an indulgent soak.

My husband knew how much I loved those fresh flowers and how much I thoroughly enjoyed them. Most of all, I was grateful for his thoughtfulness in simply remembering our special day. With that same kind of thoughtfulness, we can transform our homes into places of welcome that mirror hearts of caring.

CHAPTER THREE

The Happiness of Work

*But as for you, be strong and do not give up,
for your work will be rewarded.*

THE BOOK OF 2 CHRONICLES

ot having a goal is more to be feared than not reaching a goal. I would rather attempt to do something great and fail than to attempt to do nothing and succeed." I kept this quote in my college journal and have continued to refer to it, for I have long been a believer in setting goals. By writing my goals down and reviewing them on a daily basis, I stay reminded of where I want to go and what I want to do in both my personal and professional life.

Several years ago, I served as chairperson of our church bazaar. I thought it would be fun to raffle off a quilt to raise money for the missions our ladies' group supported.

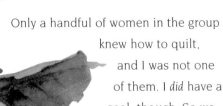

Only a handful of women in the group knew how to quilt, and I was not one of them. I *did* have a goal, though. So we set a meeting time of once a week to work on our project. Each week, we faithfully gathered to piece and stitch our quilt, and miraculously finished it one day before the bazaar. Our prize was admired by all who attended the bazaar's turkey dinner, and the winner of the quilt was the star of the evening. The raffle was so well-received that it became a yearly tradition.

Our grand business in life is not to see what lies dimly at a distance, but to do what lies clearly at hand.
THOMAS CARLYLE

Ten years later, the ladies of my church still meet once a week to work on a quilt for our annual November bazaar. Pieces of cloth are lovingly cut out, arranged, and stitched together to form a beautiful masterpiece. Week after week, the women faithfully work on their creation. One year, they made a Log Cabin quilt, another year a Wedding Ring. This year it was a bow-tie design. It is still the highlight of the bazaar to see who will win the quilt.

Immediately after the quilt is presented to the winner, the quilting circle ladies begin to plan the next year's prize. A year's worth of work brings more than a year's worth of joy to these ladies who set their goal and reach it time after time. Not only is the finished quilt a wonder to behold, but the weekly gatherings of friends who work on the quilt is a reward in itself. Potluck is the standard lunchtime fare, and recipes are traded freely. Along with each stitch, the women share their joys, cares,

Little Blessings of Work

Whether you work in an office or at home, strive to be a blessing to others in the little things you do. Here are some ideas to get you started.

- ❧ Run an errand for someone who doesn't drive.
- ❧ Give a soft drink to a repair person.
- ❧ Keep hand sanitizer in your purse and in the car, especially during cold and flu season, and share it at the office.
- ❧ Carry wrapped hard candies to sweeten someone's day.
- ❧ Write thank-you notes.
- ❧ Say *please, thank you,* and *excuse me.* They're words of respect.
- ❧ Buy two nice ink pens and share one with someone at work as a thoughtful gesture.
- ❧ Put the fire out on gossip when you see it smoking.
- ❧ Offer to start a birthday calendar for a group of friends or relatives.
- ❧ Create a lost-and-found basket at work.
- ❧ Help someone when he or she least expects it.
- ❧ When at work, treat your job as the most important thing you do.

and concerns. And the goals they reach are lofty ones. Not only do they finish the quilt, but the process brings friends together week after week, welcomes newcomers to the circle, and enriches the lives of each of these women who share a common goal.

I never did anything worth doing by accident, nor did any of my inventions come by accident, they came by work.
THOMAS EDISON

Did you know that even the most mundane of tasks can be meaningful? I was recently made aware of that when my oldest son told me that he used to love watching me iron. When he was little, he so enjoyed talking to me while I ironed, for I was actually in one place long enough for him to have my undivided attention. I couldn't believe that he looked back on my ironing as a memorable event. However, as a young mother, I took pleasure in ironing my husband's shirts, for they smelled of the man I loved. Smoothing the cloth with my fingers and watching the wrinkles disappear at the tip of the iron was rewarding in itself. For my son, it was a gift of my time, something memorable being created from out of the ordinary.

My sister-in-law has the most beautiful old-fashioned flowers that grow in her yard as tall as the fence. Their purple blossoms attract not only hummingbirds and butterflies, they also

attracted me. I told her that when the flowers put forth
seeds at the end of the summer, I would love to have
some. She never forgot my request, and one fall day she

> *Whoever sows sparingly will also reap sparingly,*
> *and whoever sows generously will also reap generously.*
> **THE BOOK OF 2 CORINTHIANS**

handed me an envelope with tiny black seeds inside.
I was so thrilled as I accepted the envelope from her,
looking forward to sowing its contents in my garden.

In the early spring, I chose a special corner of the garden to sow my seeds in. Helped along by a little rain and
some weeding, these wonderful flowers are now billowing
in my yard, too. And to think they started from just tiny
black seeds!

*It is not doing the thing we like, but liking
the thing we have to do that makes life happy.*
GOETHE

Any abundant harvest begins with the planting of
seeds, and that is what work is to me—an opportunity to
sow my own variety of seeds, nurture and care for them,
and finally enjoy their bounty.

My father is eighty-seven and blessed with basically
good health. I live nearby, and I called him last week to
see if he wanted to go to the store with me. He said he'd
better not; he was just too busy right then. Even at his
age, he still has a wonderful sense of purpose to his days.
All of his working life, he was a carpenter by trade. Since
he retired, he has kept the saws in his woodworking shop
humming. Daddy never
went to college, but he

became a master of his work anyway. He knew that his God-given talents were in his hands.

Work is a blessing, and for us to receive blessings we must find work.

ALDA

Even now, antique shop owners still bring him an assortment of furniture to fix, such as three-legged chairs, rockers with broken spindles, and all sorts of other projects, some of which are unrecognizable for what they are until he finishes with them. His reward is not just in getting paid for the work he has done. His greater reward is in seeing something made whole again and seeing the owner of the object's delight in the revival of a treasure.

With every dawning of the day come new opportunities for us. With every sunrise, we are given the gift of a new morning. It is up to us to use the talents God has given us. Some may consider work a burden, but for those of us who find it a blessing, we find many additional blessings in a job well done.

The Book of Genesis tells us how God created the heavens and the earth. God created light and He saw that it was good. After each of His creations, He looked back and saw that His day's work was good. When we finish our work, it is important that we look back at it and ask ourselves, "Is it good?" If we can answer in the affirmative, that is the greatest accomplishment of all.

CHAPTER FOUR

The Happiness of Personal Enrichment

For this very reason, make every effort to add to your faith goodness; and to goodness, knowledge.

THE BOOK OF 2 PETER

There is a familiar saying that we are never too old to learn. I love that thought! With each sunrise, the promise of a new day begins, and our world is filled with new doors of discovery. It is up to us to open them and step inside.

Reading is a sure way to open up new avenues of discovery. Newspapers, books, and magazines are full of creative ideas on everything from entertaining to crafting to dog grooming. We can improve and inspire every facet of our lives as we discover new ways to clean our homes, solve family problems, or even launch a new business. We can explore health issues and learn about charities that need our support.

I have created a library in our home
with books on all sorts of topics,
from horses to antiques to my
son's favorite series, C.S. Lewis'
Chronicles of Narnia.

A cozy chair with a quilt draped
over its arm and a good reading lamp are symbols of
quiet pleasure, unique emblems of home. Give me a cup
of tea and a good book, and I am ready to settle in. I love
the softness of quilts, and they are especially wonderful
when they are family treasures. Simple, elegant, and
uniquely American, quilts are ideal props to inspire a
reading corner.

Education was most important to my mother. She
used to say, "I could finish
school, but I could never
finish my education."
Because she had grown up
during the Great Depression,
she liked to add, "Nor could it
ever be taken away from me."

Every spring and fall,
our city newspaper
lists a

A Helping Hand

When you close your eyes at night, it's good to ask yourself, "Did I help someone today?" Chances are, you did! If you're looking to add some personal enrichment to your life, here are some ideas to ponder.

- Perform a simple act of kindness for someone you know. Give a neighbor a call to check on her. Run an errand for a shut-in. Send a meal to someone who is ill. Write a letter of encouragement to a friend. Donate some clothing to a women's shelter.

- Read about organizations such as Greenpeace and the Sierra Club. Become educated on ways to preserve the environment for the next generation.

- Become involved in your child's education. Schools always need parent helpers, and volunteering helps you feel more connected to your child. My son's school has a rummage sale that I help out with each year. The chairman of the sale committee has a son who attended school there twenty years ago, and the dad is still active in his son's school!

- You can read a book to learn something new, or you can learn in a more unconventional way. Search the Internet for fun self-education tools like virtual tours of world-famous museums. Join a club or group that shares your interests. Expand your horizons in countless ways on your journey to personal enrichment.

- If you know a mother who has small children, offer to babysit for her free of charge. The gift of time alone is priceless to mothers with frayed nerves. The children will enjoy a change of pace, and the mother will be most grateful for your thoughtfulness.

- Offer to keep an eye on a neighbor's house while the family is away on a trip. Pick up their newspaper and mail and take care of their pets. Security on the home front provides great peace of mind to travelers.

- Send a birthday card to someone who might not be expecting it. Slip an herbal tea bag into the envelope. Everyone loves to feel special and remembered. It works wonders in breaking down barriers and forging friendships.

- Escape from the ordinary and surprise the man in your life by adding little niceties to his day—an herbal shaving cream, a soothing foot lotion, a magazine about his favorite hobby, a luscious almond soap in his shower, a nicely straightened sock drawer.

schedule of classes that are open to the community. There are so many to choose from and the cost is so minimal. I would love to take Music Appreciation, Landscaping 101, American Gourmet, French Pastry, or

> *Flowers preach to us if we will hear.*
> CHRISTINA ROSSETTI

even Welding. The list is so varied that I want to take every one of them, for it is in my spirit to know a little bit about a whole lot of things. As a wife, mother, and business owner, I just never seem to find the time to sign up for a class. But someday I will.

Before I had children, I took classes in pottery, painting, and even a powder puff mechanics course. In the mechanics course, we learned how to change a tire, fill the windshield wiper fluid, put water in the battery, and check the oil of our cars. I am most grateful to have a husband who faithfully takes care of all that, but I have a wonderful sense of satisfaction that if I had to, I could do those things, too. I also have a sense of security in traveling far away from home and having some basic car repair knowledge under my hat.

The little nuggets of information that enrich our lives are priceless, especially when we really need them. Knowledge is so valuable, for you never know when it might come in handy. When I took the mechanics class, I probably never traveled more than fifty miles from home. Now, my work travels sometimes take me hundreds of miles away. That course from long ago has proven very useful.

My father-in-law is in his eighties and suffers terribly from the pain of arthritis. I was so proud of him when he signed up for a water aerobics class. To my surprise, he is thoroughly enjoying it. He says, "See how much straighter I am walking." And yes, he is walking with improved posture.

But the very idea of him taking an aerobics class instead of staying home and complaining is what most impressed me.

No matter what our age, a bit of personal enrichment can truly change our lives. Now Papa is walking straight and tall, and continuing his Wednesday deliveries of Meals on Wheels. He continues to bless others with his gift of volunteering. Not only does he provide shut-ins with warm food, but he also lingers a bit to engage in some warm conversation.

There are many ways in which we can lend assistance to others. Sometimes it is performing a very simple act that improves the lives of countless people. Our local Red Cross chapter just loves my husband, for his blood type is O-positive—the universal donor. He regularly gives blood and often goes in to donate when the blood bank has a special need. So many lives have been saved through all of the wonderful people who give blood.

In front of my son's school are several flowerbeds. Some are rather simple and others are overflowing with blooms. I always wondered why each flowerbed looked different from the others, and then one day I discovered little plant stakes in the beds. One read, "This flowerbed is lovingly cared for by the Palich family." Another said, "This flowerbed is lovingly cared for by the LaForest family." I learned the beds were taken care of by volunteers who gave of their time and energy to soften the schoolyard with a touch of grace and charm.

> *If any little word of mine*
> *May make some heart the lighter;*
> *If any little song of mine*
> *May make some life the brighter:*
> *God let me speak that little word*
> *And take my bit of singing*
> *And plant it in some lonely vale*
> *To set the echoes ringing.*
>
> ANONYMOUS

There are so many ways we can enrich the lives of others, and, in doing so, we are the ones most blessed. We are all given different talents and gifts. Some of us are blessed with the valuable gift of listening. Sometimes just having someone hear our problems, cares, and concerns is exactly what we need.

No matter what our interests, no matter what our gifts and talents, while we are enriching the lives of others, we

You must never find time for anything.
If you want time you must make it.

CHARLES BUXTON

will be blessed with joy and contentment ourselves.

If you don't know where to begin, look in your newspaper or call your local library. Volunteer organizations are always in need of help. The schools need people to help out in classrooms, the food bank could always use a little extra help stocking shelves and sorting canned goods, and the Red Cross often needs volunteers to work the phones. A child in your neighborhood would be thrilled to have you help him or her with homework. The rewards of this type of personal enrichment are worth far more than anyone could ever pay you. They are deposits worth countless riches in the bank of eternity.

CHAPTER FIVE

The Happiness of Faith

We live by faith, not by sight.

THE BOOK OF 2 CORINTHIANS

When I was in elementary school, a friend of our family would come and spend a weekend with us every now and then. Rose taught music at a local school and had won several teaching awards. She played the piano beautifully. I remember sitting on the piano bench alongside her and watching her fingers fly over the keys. Almost anything I requested, Rose could play—rock 'n roll, ragtime, and beautiful hymns alike would flow from her fingers, all without a note of sheet music.

During the Christmas holidays, our family bundled up and made a special trip to the Christmas pageant at

Rose's school. The children sang and acted out the nativity scene, complete with angels and cardboard sheep. After the play, Rose took us on a tour of the school and introduced us to some of her students. Rose was also a houseparent at the school, and even though most of the children were very young, several of them lived on campus. So Rose taught music by day and tucked a dorm room of third graders into bed by night.

> *Now faith is being sure of what we hope for and certain of what we do not see.*
> THE BOOK OF HEBREWS

Never married, Rose had no children of her own, only the little ones who came into her life through music. She didn't claim any family nearby, so we accepted her as a part of our own. I so looked forward to those special Friday nights when Daddy would drive over to the school to pick her up for the weekend.

Rose was a very special lady, for she taught and loved and shared her heart. She could have just as well been bitter and resentful; Rose, you see, had been blind since birth. The school that she taught at was the Arkansas School for the Blind. Her books were in Braille and she read with her fingers. She had never seen a sunrise, much less the faces of her students, but she did see the music and joy in their hearts. Through Rose's determination and faith, she overcame her obstacle and lived a joyful life.

Ways to Rekindle Your Spirit

Meditate — Devote a quiet time of the day to positive and inspirational thinking. Morning meditations can start off your day on a positive note while evening reflections can put the day's happenings into perspective.

Eliminate — Remove from your life television, movies, and videos that are negative. There is a spiritual freedom *from* it, instead of it having an influence on you.

Journal — Sometimes it helps to see all the things we are thankful for written down on paper. A friend of mine who works in a youth prison ministry asked a group of students to write down something they were thankful for. One boy simply wrote down that he was thankful for clean clothes that fit. The back door painted, the lost family dog found, a job secured, a friendship mended, a lease signed—no matter what the day brings, it is full of blessings.

Set Goals — I like to write down exactly what my goals are. I keep a one-year plan and a five-year plan. It helps me to review them daily. If I feel sure in knowing where I want to go, I can develop a plan of action to help me reach my goals.

Get Support — Take care of your soul by surrounding yourself with others who are genuinely and sincerely encouraging. Support groups are life changing for some. Attending church is nourishing to my spirit, for not only do I receive the message of inspiration and hope by listening to the message, I am also surrounded by a community of church family who loves and supports my own family and me. Sitting alongside my husband and sons in the oak pew is a comforting way to bring to a close the end of the week and open the door on a Monday morning.

All the beautiful sentiments in the world weigh less than a single lovely action.

JAMES RUSSELL LOWELL

There is truth in the saying that the things that count most in life are the things that cannot be counted. Rose had very little money, no family, and eyes that could not see. But anyone who knew Rose could tell you that she was rich—rich in her upbeat, optimistic, and enthusiastic spirit.

Happiness is like ripples on the water.
It spreads to all who surround you.
ALDA

To this day, Rose has been an inspiration to me as I strive to emulate her approach to life and her wonderful attitude. She showed me that no matter what life gives me, how I handle it is what will make the difference. My faith has taught me that happiness is not in the absence of problems but in the ability to deal with them. Disappointments and setbacks will cloud our lives, no matter how much we are blessed with. We have the choice to be thankful or resentful. I can fuss with the thorns on the rose bush, or be thankful that the thorn bush has roses.

Helen Keller once said, "If the outlook is not good, try the up look. It is always good." That has been a wonderful bit of advice for me, as my life has been touched by cancer, experienced the heartache of losing a loved one, and seen plenty of disappointment. Yet my faith has always given me strength. The sun has set on yesterday. I have been given the gift of today and the hope of tomorrow.

A Day Remembered

The Lord is my shepherd, I shall not be in want.
He makes me lie down in green pastures,
he leads me beside quiet waters,
he restores my soul.

THE BOOK OF PSALMS

A longtime treasured employee of my company had her faith tested when she lost everything in a tornado last year. Liz lost all of her clothes, furniture, and family treasures, as everything inside her house was blown outside. Three people were killed in her neighborhood, and the devastation was estimated to be in millions of dollars in our city. Trees were splinted like toothpicks. Only a concrete slab was left where a huge grocery store had once stood. Somehow through it all, Liz and her son managed to escape injury as they huddled in a closet. Liz tells of the moments of terror and of how she

and her son fervently prayed all the while glass, wood, and steel whirled about them.

Months have passed since the tornado struck, and slowly Liz has rebuilt her home. Friends at work have helped her with gifts of clothes, pillows, sheets, and blankets. The most amazing thing of all is that when Liz talks about that terrible day and all of her losses, she never once complains. She simply ends the story by telling people how fortunate she was to be protected and to have friends help restore her possessions and get her settled into a new home. The most important thing in her life was her son, and he was safe in her arms. If you ask Liz what kept her from being blown away, she will tell you it was simply her faith. It was never blown away.

With determination, a courageous attitude, and our faith, we can be happy in the worst of circumstances, for they enable us to easily evaluate what is truly important in our lives. The things it takes to make us happy—friends, family, home, work, personal interests, and, most of all, faith—are blessings of a heart full of happiness. May life bring you love, peace, hope, happiness, and all that is good.